Sacred Sex

Barbara Lee

To John! Thanks for all you do for our young people! You are an inspiration. Namaste! Barbara Lee

Sacred Sex

Published by

ISBN 978-1-939294-18-0

Dedication

To Leif

For slowing me down
to the speed of life.

Acknowledgments

My own experience and my experience as the pastor of an open and inclusive interfaith community has shown me the damage we suffer when the connection between our spiritual and our sexual selves is severed. I am grateful for the courage and tenacity of the many people who shared with me their own struggles to feel sexually healthy and whole. I am hopeful this small book will serve in the big mission of dismantling shame, healing wounds and preventing further harm as we joyfully claim and celebrate our sexuality.

As I was wrestling with my own internal contradictions, I received the priceless gift of guidance and instruction from my pastoral care professor, Jaco Hamman. Jaco deserves the credit for introducing me to the idea of a Sexual Ethic which is the foundation on which this book is built. I am profoundly grateful for Jaco's insights, support and friendship.

While all of the elements of this book were rambling around in my head and shared in bits and pieces with others, it was my editor and publisher, Tricia L. McDonald, who read my work and felt it was worth sharing with a wider audience. I am deeply indebted to Tricia for encouraging me to take the important step of publication and for providing the assistance and knowledge I have depended upon throughout the process.

I also need to acknowledge my family who never cease to amaze me with their love and support. For putting up with my long nights and days caring for others as they were growing up, I will be forever in the debt of my sons Jackson and Alex. For remaining always in my heart even after leaving my arms too soon, I am grateful to my son Malachi. For giving me every day the gift of joy that comes from one who recognizes her own beauty, I thank my "significant daughter" Brigid. Finally, I need to express my deepest gratitude to my life partner Leif Van Horssen with whom I find my deepest peace in being my most authentic self.

Table of Contents

Lovers/At Night We Fall

The minute I heard my first love story
I started looking for you, not knowing
How blind that was.
Lovers don't finally meet somewhere.
They're in each other all along.
At night we fall into each other with such grace.
When it's light, you throw me back
Like you do your hair.
Your eyes now drunk with God,
Mine with looking at you,
One takes care of the other.
Rumi

Creating a Sexual Ethic

Pastor Will Willimon tells of the time he was preaching in a large auditorium. The introduction he received was far more than he felt his sermon deserved. But he recalled he had been told, "When a sermon is weak, say it louder." So he was loud, emotional, and passionate. "And what," he asked, "is the most significant event our faith has to offer?"

"The erection!" he bellowed. A woman in the front row screamed.

"I mean the resurrection, the resurrection," he repeated at least a dozen times – although it did no good.

The first time I spoke about sex at church, there was a young female college student in the community. My message confused her. It wasn't what she expected to hear. So when we gathered for conversation afterward she offered a rather tenuous question, and you could tell from the slight shake in her voice that she was ready to be slapped down. "Are you saying," she asked, "that sex can be okay outside of marriage?"

I hesitated. This was a direct question and there was no fancy talking around it. I looked at the people around the table, trying to gauge their reactions, and then it just came out. Yes! That is exactly what I was saying. Even now I recall how liberating that felt. No dancing around the question. And how liberating it was for that young woman, as well.

So just to get it out of the way in case you are uncertain and looking for clarification: Yes, I believe sex outside of marriage can be perfectly healthy and holy.

I also recognize that in that belief, I directly challenge both the wisdom and the constraint of our culture's current marriage ethic. Basically the marriage ethic says that if you are married, sex is acceptable and if you are not married, sex is bad. Such an ethic has nothing, however, to say to single teenagers, single gays and lesbians, single elderly, or the single disabled. In fact, it has nothing to say to anyone who isn't, well, married. At the same time it assumes that a whole host of abusive, demeaning and controlling behaviors are permissible as long as, or even because, they take place within a legally recognized union.

Another problem with using a marriage ethic to make decisions about our sexuality is that it assumes that the purpose and ultimate goal of marriage is sex, and the purpose and ultimate goal of sex is life-long bonding. Traditionally, marriage has provided an economic arrangement that included a provision for the raising of children. Will Farrell speaks of first-stage marriages as those in which women seek the most successful men and men seek the most beautiful women. Men use their financial means to secure sex while women use sex to access economic protection and to fulfill their mothering role. In both of these ways, the couple owns each other and believes they have the right to control the other's behavior. In our modern world, we are learning to relate to each other not as property but as whole human beings.

While that is a positive development, another change in our modern expectations of each other is far less so. As families and communities have broken down, we have become more and more isolated so our spouse can become our only means of emotional, spiritual and physical support. One person is now expected to not just be a partner in a living arrangement, but to also be a lover, best friend, therapist, aunt/uncle, parent, sibling, doctor and priest. Now that we are living to be as much as one hundred years old, such pressure may be exerted for seventy or eighty years. It can simply be too much weight for any one person to bear. No wonder so many marriages end in divorce.

Instead, I argue that we need to develop and live by a sexual ethic that places sexuality in the context of the divine and treats it with moral integrity. Such an ethic begins by recognizing that people of all sexual orientations and gender identities, of all marital status and of all physical capacities, have the right to experience sex as a healthy and life giving part of their existence. Crafting a sexual ethic requires us to bring intentionality and discernment to our sexual decisions. In order for sex to be healthy and holy, we must begin by recognizing that sex engages us completely, both body and soul.

Notes:_____

_____

_____

_____

_____

_____

_____

_____

_____

_____

_____

_____

_____

_____

_____

_____

_____

_____

_____

Sex and Scripture

There is a wonderful model for such a sexual ethic in Christian scripture. In the passionate words of the *Song of Songs*, we find a compelling and graphic witness to the beauty of the human body, the goodness of sexual desire, and the power of love.

This book describes a non-marital sexual relationship without procreative purpose. So how did this get into the Bible? That's a question that has long been debated. As an easy out, many religious leaders have said that this erotic love poem is actually an analogy of God's love for God's people. That may be, but there is no denying that this is also a song about human desire.

The *Song of Songs* is a poem about a black and beautiful woman and a radiant and ruddy man as they speak the language of longing, celebrating every inch of each other's bodies, every smell and every taste. Describing a moment when her lover knocked on her door and she hesitated to open it, the woman speaks some of the most erotic lines you'll find in any literature:

My beloved thrust his hand into the opening,
And my inmost being yearned for him.
I arose to open to my beloved,
And my hands dripped with myrrh,
My fingers with liquid myrrh,
Upon the handles of the bolt.

When she opens the door he is gone. "I adjure you, O daughters of Jerusalem," she says, "If you find my beloved, tell him this: I am faint with love."

Ultimately, the *Song of Songs* is a book of hope because we so often need to be convinced of the goodness of our bodies. We so often need to have our desire for intimate touch answered by the touch of another.

But how many churches use this text to educate young people, or old people, about the exquisite value of sexual ecstasy? St. Bernard of Clairvaux even counseled that young monks and nuns were not to read the book until their faith had matured because of the sexual feelings it was capable of inspiring.

We can give much credit for our sexual hang-ups and taboos within the Christian tradition to St. Augustine, who lived around 400AD and who is credited with the idea of original sin. St. Augustine found himself in a continual battle with his own unwanted sexual energy, leading him to conclude that sex was the sin of Adam. This part of our human nature was so primitive, he concluded, that we have no mental or spiritual control over it, and it is thus original sin.

Augustine thought that sexual intercourse was just as bad and uncontrollable whether one was married or not, but that an excuse could be made for it within marriage because then it served the purpose of producing legitimate children. However, even marital sex still provided the way in which original sin was passed from father to child as both guilt for Adam's crime and the sickness or defect that gives human beings a sinful nature.

Today a number of sexual taboos have been lifted and many people, even unmarried people, are having, and presumably enjoying, sex. Yet despite these cultural shifts, we still hear the church largely echoing St. Augustine's doctrine: Sex is dangerous. Sexual desire is wrong. Female sexuality is destructive and evil. Male sexuality is predatory and uncontrollable. It is the task of every civilized human being to confine sexuality within very narrow limits.

Negative social conditioning about sex inevitably creates fear, and this fear is passed on from generation to generation by well-intentioned parents, teachers, and religious leaders. In early childhood, most of us absorb disapproving attitudes about sex without even becoming aware of the process. As a result, we can find ourselves struggling with our ability to express our own sexuality, and to love and open up to another.

The warnings are all around us: Watch out! If you open up to love and sex more fully, you will get hurt.

When I was growing up those narrow limits meant that the only place it was appropriate to even consider sex was within marriage. Sex for any other reason or in any other circumstance was simply wrong. That lesson and the veil of guilt it draped over me kept me from having important conversations with trusted elders, including my mother, about my own blossoming sexuality. That conditioning led me to make some pretty devastating choices in my life.

My problem was not that I had sex with a lot of people, it was that I felt compelled to marry everyone I had sex with. I was in a Catch-22. Because of my childhood experiences of sexual abuse and the social messaging all around me, I didn't think anyone would be interested in me if I didn't make myself sexually available to them. And once I had sex, I was so overwhelmed with guilt that the only way to make things better was to get married. In a world of so many mixed messages, we NEED to be willing to talk about sex openly, honestly and above all realistically, and we especially need to talk about it in church and with our young people.

Notes:_____

_____

_____

_____

_____

_____

_____

_____

_____

_____

_____

_____

_____

_____

_____

_____

_____

_____

_____

_____

_____

Our Sexual Bodies

The first lesson is that sex is a good gift of God. We are all sexual beings and our bodies, no matter the size, shape, age or condition, are beautiful. To believe that God doesn't like sex is like believing that God doesn't like you. With that kind of foundation, we are almost certain to end up carrying shame for our own perfectly natural sexual desires and fulfillments. It doesn't have to be that way. In the book *The Ethical Slut* a woman shares her story of discovering the joys of masturbation as a young girl, in the back seat of the family car tucked under a warm blanket on a long trip. It felt so wonderful that she concluded the existence of her clitoris was proof positive that God loved her.

Sex serves a lot of purposes. Procreation is one. Pleasure is another. Feeling accepted, loved and finding emotional fulfillment is yet another.

Beyond that, sex can play a role in our spirituality. David Scherer, the hip-hop artist who performs as *Agape* at Christian gatherings around the country sent me an email about this topic. In it he wrote, "I have trouble embracing a philosophy that creates dualism with spirit and flesh. I think sensuality is something wonderful that is not to be freed from, but engaged and integrated into our spirituality. In fact, I'd say it already is if we want it to be or not. That is one of the bones for me to pick with Christianity…some people seem to really ignore the Jewish understanding of spirituality being what we do with our bodies, not just concepts to think about."

David Deida describes three stages of sexual relationships. The first is getting what we want and feeling good. "As long as you give me what I want, everything will be fine." The second stage moves beyond "what's in it for me" to embrace true mutuality and equality. It's a place of negotiation and making deals for the sake of the relationship. But beyond feeling good or making the relationship work is a third stage that recognizes sex as something that breaks you open to the Spirit and to the world so that intimate communion is not only a blessing for two people, but for all of their relationships and for all beings.

The way we use our bodies is an expression of spirituality. We may make the choice to express our spirituality by practicing celibacy. Such a decision is absolutely valid and commendable. Despite overwhelming cultural messages to the contrary, we can be whole without a sexual partner, and all of the world's religious traditions have seen value in claiming this way of life.

There are other ways to use our bodies to express our spirituality: dancing, athletics, fasting and feasting are just some examples. Yet another way is by pursuing the path of sexual transcendence in which we move outside the boundaries of our individual selves to receive this world in a way that is motivated by love and speaks of God's own passionate creativity.

Martin Amis describes his experience of his wife making love to him at a time when he felt ugly and unlovable. He writes "The next morning I woke early and lay there quietly laughing and weeping into the pillow. I felt fragile, guileless, and exquisitely consoled."

I love that description of how we are rendered by good sex with a loving partner. We are left with a sense of fragility and vulnerability having risked exposing ourselves so fully to each other. We are left feeling guileless because we have allowed our masks and self-deceptions to fall away. We are left exquisitely consoled because we have experienced our desire met while also satisfying the desire of another.

But sex alone is no guarantee of such intimacy. For sex can only be exquisitely consoling and reflective of God's desire for us when two people make themselves vulnerable to each other. It cannot be had when one person is being exploited. It cannot be had when love is withheld. It cannot be had when it is being used as a means to any other end than mutual reverence and delight. What a fine line there is between sex that heals and sex that wounds.

Notes:_____

_____

_____

_____

_____

_____

_____

_____

_____

_____

_____

_____

_____

_____

_____

_____

_____

_____

_____

_____

_____

A Sexual Ethic

The human animal is the only one that can direct their sexual energy wherever they want. Some choose to use this energy in life-giving, celebrating and enriching ways. Some choose to use this energy in abusive and negative ways. Others waste it and disperse it indiscriminately. There are many ways in which we can express sexual energy, both positively and negatively. Sex between people who do not love one another and are not willing to become uniquely responsible to and for one another assumes a split between body and spirit that does not exist. When we have sex, all of who we are is on the line. Any attempt to divide the body and the spirit does violence to both.

There is so much of that happening in our world today. One minute our culture is seeking to exploit sex, demean it and turn it into a sport.

The next minute our society is trying to repress it, even vilify it. How do we find our own way through the confusing and contradictory messages of our time? How do we advise our children and others who struggle with questions of sexuality? Negotiating our sex lives can be incredibly difficult. In our encounters with desire, we might entrust ourselves to someone who is not careful with our bodies or our spirits. Bad sexual experience is so wounding, so difficult to recover from.

Hence, it is long overdue that we develop and live by a sexual ethic. Crafting a sexual ethic requires us to bring intentionality and discernment to our sexual decisions. We cannot create a sexual ethic in the heat of the moment. We need to take time to reflect on how we will be sexual beings in this world. We need to create a sexual ethic that takes seriously the desires, needs and pains of our bodies. So what are the elements of a sexual ethic?

A sexual ethic begins by insisting that mutual **consent** is imperative in each and every sexual interaction. Both people must have the option of saying "yes" but also the opportunity to say "no," and to do so without being punished. Consent is never the same as submitting, going along with or acquiescing. Authentic consent requires communication and agreement that no means no, yes means yes and maybe means maybe. "No" will not be punished by withdrawal or coercive tactics. "Maybe" requires waiting for "yes" without manipulation or pushing.

Certainly, any sexual encounter also requires a degree of spiritual and emotional **maturity**. Rather than prescribing to an arbitrary age of consent, an individual must be able to reasonably and honestly reflect upon their situation. Maturity brings with it a secure **self-identity**. The teenage years are especially rife with the angst of trying to discover who one is. Many of our sons and daughters are searching desperately for who they are. They will not find themselves in sex. We also have times of doubt and wonder when we question who we are. Likewise, we will not find ourselves in sex. However, when we begin our sexual encounters with a healthy grasp of who we are, we can deepen and even evolve our understanding of our own identity.

The next part of a sexual ethic involves entering into sexual intimacy only when the power, and subsequently the vulnerability, of two people are **equal**. We will certainly experience sexual feelings toward persons who have more or less power than we possess, but whether we pursue those feelings is always a choice. To engage in a sexual relationship with someone in a position of power over us is to increase our risk of being taken advantage of. To pursue such a relationship with someone less powerful than us means we risk taking advantage of another.

A sexual ethic clearly requires taking **responsibility** for protecting oneself and one's partner from sexually transmitted disease and unplanned pregnancy. This cannot be accomplished effectively while in the act or the morning after. Instead, it requires the kind of respect and communication between two people that is borne out of care, both for one's own needs and for the well-being of one's partner.

Shared sexual expression requires **relational intimacy**, knowing someone over time and sharing a history in which trust has developed. It requires that one be faithful to their promises. Whatever the nature of commitment to a partner and whatever the duration of that commitment, it must be anchored in fidelity. Individuals may change in ways that change the commitment they are willing to make, but those changes need to be addressed through open and honest communication. People can only enter into those discussions if there is first and foremost a faithfulness rooted in truthfulness, dependability and promise-keeping.

Expressing our sexuality must be both **other-enriching** and **self-liberating**. Our sexual choices must demonstrate a generous interest and concern for the well-being of the other. Sacred sex is sensitive, considerate, thoughtful, compassionate, understanding and supportive. It forgives, heals and calls forth the best from the other. While sexuality is a gift we give, there must also be an element of wholesome self-interest as we also receive the gifts of sexual expression.

Finally, a sexual ethic involves appreciation of the **joyous** gift of life and the mystery of love. We should never allow sex to become a mere passive duty of submission or a heartless conformity to expectation. The element of the erotic, instinctual desire for pleasure and gratification deserves to be affirmed and encouraged. Human sexual expression is meant to be enjoyed as a passionate celebration without feelings of guilt or remorse.

Notes:_____

_____

_____

_____

_____

_____

_____

_____

_____

_____

_____

_____

_____

_____

_____

_____

_____

_____

_____

_____

Sexual Beings

Over the past 2,000 years there has been a needless divorce between Christian spirituality and natural sexuality. But if we genuinely believe in incarnational theology, then we will seek to practice living our lives in such a way that we treat our bodily selves as a good gift from God. And we will affirm that sexual pleasure is also good. A sexual ethic encourages us not to meet our own sexual needs at the expense of someone else. It also recognizes that there are no simple answers and no permanent resolutions, but that we enter into a constant process of ethical discernment. That is an enormous head start as we negotiate our sexuality today.

The *Song of Songs* describes a wonderful, passionate relationship that reverences the gift of sexuality. The lovers are evenly matched in the force of their desire. They are equally vulnerable in their desire to be desired by the other. They are equally determined to give and to receive pleasure. Here, desire doesn't lead to exploitation or abuse but to full participation of the body in the world.

The *Song* shows us a path, through desire, outside the boundaries of our individual selves, because it offers a way of receiving the world that is motivated by love and speaks of God's own passionate creativity. It teaches that in seeking the pleasure of another we may find our own deepest pleasure and in commitment to another we may come to know ecstasy.

It is when we bring the Spirit back to sex, that we can honor our sexuality as a bridge between the body and the soul. When combined with love, sexual energy is the most powerful stimulus of all, a rich treasure of joy, happiness and passion. But it remains a virtue only to the degree that it is used with wisdom, compassion and understanding. With this powerful force comes a responsibility to use the extra energy gained in loving and positive ways.

In her book *Radical Wisdom: A Feminist Mystical Theology*, Beverly Lanzetta writes, "As sexual beings, our creativity and passion are not separate from the mystical or contemplative, but expressions of the mutual interpenetration, co-equality and co-intimacy that exist between spirit and body...sexual love can be viewed as a type of infused contemplation. Here there is fusion – an intimate dance of spirit and body... Whether sexual intimacy is lived out through physical intercourse, spiritual love, or unimagined expressions of human creativity, it overflows from our core of goodness and generosity in loving imitation of how God loves."

The Taoists observed that the way of nature is interactive and full of creative, life-giving, sexual energy. Rain penetrates the earth, giving birth to trees and flowers; rivers caress rocks; the ocean plunges into the sand; and the sunshine is absorbed into the womb of the earth, giving birth to all life. Sexual energy is the creative force that permeates the universe. Life springs forth from balancing sexual energies through the combination of yin and yang.

In *The Art of Sexual Ecstasy*, author Margot Anand reflects that, "The desire to unite sexually with another human being is a reflection of our underlying spiritual need to experience wholeness and complete intimacy, transcending the individual's sense of separateness and isolation. It is a need to return to the original source of creation, to the oneness we experienced in our mother's womb and beyond that to a oneness within the self."

Sexual union without this sacred element rarely satisfies our needs and then only does so fleetingly. But with the sacred element added, it is possible for us to experience a connection with the life force itself, with our deepest creative impulses. Vikas Malkani, an Indian spiritual guide and author writes, "Making love can become a giving, expressing, selfless act, which is a form of prayer in itself. Through the body, the hearts are touched; the emotions opened, needs and desires expressed, fears released, security given and souls merged. Through the act of physical sharing, God is revered and remembered. Making love goes from the physical to the emotional and finally to the spiritual level where it becomes a prayer to the Divine."

Sexuality as a sacred practice is about trusting, receiving and penetrating each other completely. It is about the circulation of energy and divine light from your body into your partner's. It is, in the words of David Deida, "the ongoing communion of consciousness and light."

In that union with each other and with the Divine, we create and emit energy that has holy power. Sacred sex is a portal through which we experience Divine love and then offer that love back so it infuses all of our relationships and sanctifies the world.

Notes:_____

_____

_____

_____

_____

_____

_____

_____

_____

_____

_____

_____

_____

_____

_____

_____

_____

_____

_____

Inclusive Sex

Jim has been with his partner for thirty-five years, and this fall he will marry his soul mate, Craig. It's legal in Massachusetts. His partner will walk down the aisle, and Jim will roll down the aisle with the help of an electric wheelchair. They will stand in their church before their friends and family and exchange their vows. They will pledge to continue the commitment they started thirty-five years ago. And a pastor will pronounce them legally wed.

But it won't be their pastor. It will be a friendly United Church of Christ pastor from the same part of town. I'm sure he's a nice man. He is a pastor after all. But he's not Jim's pastor, because Jim's pastor is ordained in a church that does not recognize or condone same sex marriage. Jim's pastor talked to his bishop and asked for permission to perform this ceremony, but he was told it wouldn't be right, it would send the wrong message. Jim's pastor had no choice but to tell Jim to wait, maybe the church will decide, in time, that his relationship can be blessed, but not today.

After waiting thirty-five years, Jim and his partner are simply not going to wait any longer. They are going to be married, and it will be a day of joy, and it will be a day to shed a tear.

Today the topic of sexuality has to include people of all sexual orientations and gender identities. For those not familiar with the alphabet soup, it includes GLBTQIA. G for gay men like Jim and his partner Craig. L for lesbians like Misty, a youth pastor in the church she grew up in. When she came out to her youth group, they embraced and supported her. But when the group's parents found out, she was quickly fired. B for bisexuals like Joan, who is young, strong and determined to be honest about who she is. T for transgendered people like Rev. Dr. Erin Swensen, who is the only transgender person to successfully transition on the job as a pastor in a major denomination. Q for questioning or queer like Eli, who came out to his state choir group one night on tour and discovered two members had left by morning because they were too uncomfortable knowing who he really was. I for intersex, those born with chromosomal abnormalities that may produce ambiguous genitalia. I includes Alex, who struggles to find any place that feels like home. And A for allies: straight friends, family and strangers who are standing beside those they care about while standing up for justice. A includes people like Lindsey, who was dismayed at how quickly and vehemently her friends turned against a beloved female professor when they found out her partner was a woman.

Notes:_____

_____

_____

_____

_____

_____

_____

_____

_____

_____

_____

_____

_____

_____

_____

_____

_____

_____

_____

_____

_____

Sex Education

I am grateful to my mother for all the things she taught me. I am grateful to my fifth grade homeroom teacher, my seventh grade English teacher and my high school media production teacher. But some of the most important lessons, the most interesting and discussion-worthy lessons I ever received came from another source. For teaching me the things no one else wanted to talk about or even knew how to talk about, for discussing them with compassion and honesty and frankness, for keeping a sense of humor while providing me with profound insights, for all of that and more I am grateful to … Phil Donohue.

Long before talk shows became a series of loud, embarrassing family fights and blatant attempts to shame and humiliate guests and studio audience participants, Phil was exploring the nooks and crannies in our society no one else seemed to be giving any attention. Did he ever exploit people? Did he sometimes work the ratings? I'm sure he did. Maybe you never liked Phil, yourself. But to me, as a kid just trying to figure out her own identity, Phil Donohue always seemed sincere and genuine. He cared about people, and he introduced me to a whole lot of people I learned to care about, too.

It was on Phil Donohue that I learned about something called a sex change operation, and I even learned how it was done (although technology has advanced since then). More than that, it was on Phil Donohue that I met people, people who were hurting deep inside with the issue of gender identity.

I don't know about your homes, but I know we didn't talk about such things at my supper table. In fact, my mother withheld information from me that scared her. In order to lay a foundation from which to have our birds-and-bees talks, she used a series of books, each written for a different age level. She didn't give me the high school level book until after I had graduated and moved out. She had kept this book away from me because it included a discussion of homosexuality, and she didn't trust that I was ready for that information.

We also didn't talk about such things at school. And heaven forbid we should ever talk about such things at church. This silence kept a lot of people comfortable. And it created and perpetuated a living hell for countless others.

Phil Donohue did not create the secrets others kept to themselves; instead, he exposed them to public light. Meanwhile in the background, his wife Marlo Thomas and her friends were singing:

There's a land that I see where
the children are free
And I say it ain't far to this land
from where we are…
where you and me are free to be
you and me.

That recording was released in 1972, over forty years ago. Maybe that land was a little further away than either Marlo or Phil or a much younger me could know, way back then.

Indeed, I imagine that St. Peter himself would be disturbed that some 2,000 years after his vision, a direct revelation that he received from God, the Christian community could still have the audacity to look at any human being and not see them as God's good creation, pure and holy in God's sight.

The vision came to Peter as he wrestled with the chief concern of a newfound Christian community: Where do Gentiles belong? And the conclusion was clear. Peter says, "You are well aware that it is against our law for a Jew to associate with a Gentile or visit them. But God has shown me that **I should not call any person impure or unclean**."

The basic message of Christianity has always been one of inclusivity and love. To love one another means to genuinely care for one another, not to see each other as projects or issues or causes, but as people. People with the same trials and tribulations, failings and flaws, gifts and abilities, joys and celebrations that I experience. And in recognizing my own limitations, I know with utter certainty that I can no longer sit in judgment of anyone else for any reason at all. Our call is simply to love, to believe in and to serve each other.

We haven't reached the land where all people are free yet, but thank God it's getting closer!

Today people are starting to share their secrets, to come out of the closet they have hidden in or been forced into for years. Today people who care have formed organizations like GIFT (Gays in Faith Together) and PFLAG (Parents and Friends of Lesbians and Gays) to provide support for themselves and to educate the rest of us. Today, communities of faith, churches for heaven's sake, can talk not in muted whispers but in loud resounding voices about sexuality and sexual identity.

Notes:_____

_____

_____

_____

_____

_____

_____

_____

_____

_____

_____

_____

_____

_____

_____

_____

_____

_____

_____

_____

_____

Spiritual Violence

Unfortunately, there are other voices in the church that are also talking loudly about sexuality and sexual identity, and their message is not one of love and inclusivity but of exclusion and hate. The saddest thing about the Hate Movement is there is too much to cover. Too many groups with too many vicious agendas. Too many victims of too many crimes. Too many people who have been broken by broken people and the rubble lies like broken walls around our feet.

Do we start with Tyra Hunter, who was injured in a car accident and was treated by emergency personnel – until they discovered she was transgender? Tyra died a short time later when a doctor at the hospital she was taken to also refused to treat her. Do we begin with Matthew Shepherd, the famous Laramie, Colorado victim? Matthew died after being beaten and tied to a fence while his tears washed a path down his blood-covered face. Do we begin with any of the more than 2,000 victims of sex-related hate crimes committed in the year 2011? They include the 18-year-old gay man from Texas allegedly slain by a classmate who feared a potential sexual advance from another man, the 31-year-old transgender woman from Pennsylvania found dead with a pillow around her head, and the 24-year-old lesbian from Florida who was purportedly killed by her girlfriend's father because he disapproved of their relationship.

Over and over I am brought to tears as I read reports of violent assaults and murders. Over and over again I am dismayed at the number of hate crimes in this country and mystified by the fact that my fellow human beings intimidate and threaten, rob and harm other people, simply because they are different.

The American Psychological Association says that hate crime is "not only an attack on one's physical self, but it is also an attack on one's very identity." People fall victim to such an attack because of how they look, how they pray or how they behave. The FBI compiles Hate Crime Statistics every year. The year 2010 marked the first year that hate crimes were declining while sexuality-related hate crimes continued to rise. Of course, everyone believes there are many more crimes that are never reported.

We could devote an entire book to these hate crimes and those who commit them. But our focus is on another kind of hate in action. This kind of hate never makes it to the FBI hate crime statistics, and is not punishable in any way. Because it is, in fact, legal.

It is spiritual violence, perpetrated against God's gay, lesbian, bisexual, transgender, queer and intersex children. It is an assault against the very spirit and soul of children of God. It is taught in pulpits around this country. It is asserted in editorials. It is found in magazines, books, television programs and political speeches. And it is a primary source of suffering for many of God's children. In fact, some members of society have used these teachings as a license to kill. Sometimes these teachings become a motive for people to kill themselves.

In a 2004 article in *Christianity Today* Harold O.J. Brown, Professor of Theology at Reformed Theological Seminary in North Carolina, wrote, "The Supreme Court, in declaring all sodomy laws unconstitutional, has in effect" (and this is in all capital letters) "DECLARED THE NATION PAGAN." If this is the way Christians behave, bring on Paganism. I won't quote him further, as his words are so ugly and offensive that they do not merit a repeat printing.

In the same issue came this sorry news: "The Roman Catholic Communion war has extended from abortion to so-called gay rights. After a bishop in Minnesota said he would not deny Communion to gay-rights supporters during Mass on Pentecost Sunday, a group of Catholic laymen took matters into their own hands. Calling themselves the Ushers of the Eucharist, 36 laymen knelt in the center aisle at the Cathedral of St. Paul to block those who wore a rainbow sash from the altar."

The country has become sadly aware of Fred Phelps and his followers who show up with vile signs and repugnant words at funerals. But the religious community can be much more subtle and effective in their attacks on homosexuals. The Federal Marriage Amendment and other anti-gay laws can easily be traced to anti-gay religious leaders misusing Biblical text. James Dobson of Focus on the Family, Exodus and other ex-gay ministries can sound like they are advocating loving programs to bring wholeness to broken people. The idea is that people can change their orientation through religious and psychological deliverance. Such assertions are not only untrue; they are dangerous.

The American Psychiatric Association, the American Medical Association and the American Academy of Pediatrics all oppose the use of reparative or conversion therapy. The APA states, "The reality is that homosexuality is not an illness. It does not require treatment and is not changeable." It goes on to say; "The potential risks of reparative therapy are great; including depression, anxiety and self-destructive behavior, since therapists' alignment with societal prejudices against homosexuality may reinforce self-hatred already experienced by the patient."

At times the damage done is so great that it leads to suicide. This is what happened in the case of Stuart Matis, a young Mormon, who concluded that one could not be both gay and Christian. A few days before he took his life, Stuart wrote to his cousin:

The Church has no idea that as I type this letter, there are surely boys and girls on their calloused knees imploring God to free them from this pain. They hate themselves… Every waking moment of every day they must be on constant alert to not divulge any clues that will identify themselves to their peers… They are afraid of their parents. They are afraid of their Bishop. They are afraid of their friends. They have nowhere to go but to lay on their floors curled in a ball and weep themselves to sleep.

When I was doing campus ministry at our local community college, I met with a professor of philosophy. The college had recently been in the news for refusing to allow a drag show to take place on its campus. The professor welcomed me and told me he hoped my presence would have a positive impact. He shared with me that in the past year, a young student of his had come out as gay to his Christian parents. They responded to his disclosure by telling him he "should kill himself." He did.

So which is worse: physical violence or spiritual violence? One arises out of hatred and intolerance bred in a gang-like atmosphere. The other is born of anti-gay rhetoric masquerading as a message of Christ's love and the power to overcome obstacles, but that gives rise to self-hatred and encourages intolerance in Christians and non-Christians alike.

When people arm themselves with the weapon of misinformation that perpetuates intolerance and preserves heterosexual privilege, the fruits of their labor are suffering, self-hatred and wasted gifts. By ignoring the true message of the Gospel, they drive people away from Christ rather than to him. By ignoring the true message of the Gospel, they imprison themselves in anger and ignorance and miss out on God's amazing message of unconditional, life-giving love. How sad for those teachers of hate. How sad for the victims of lies and intolerance.

Notes:_____

_____

_____

_____

_____

_____

_____

_____

_____

_____

_____

_____

_____

_____

_____

_____

_____

_____

_____

_____

Other Voices

I learned about Soulforce in Minnesota. It is a grassroots movement committed to nonviolence that seeks to apply the principles of Gandhi and Martin Luther King Jr. to the struggle for justice. One of the things I find striking about this ministry is the attention they pay to their adversaries. These are their beliefs:

1. My adversary is also a child of the Creator.

2. My adversary is not my enemy, but a victim of misinformation, as I have been.

3. My only task is to bring my adversary truth in love nonviolently, relentlessly.

4. My adversary's motives are as pure as mine and are of no relevance to our discussion.

5. My worst adversary has an amazing potential for positive change.

This is the promise of the Gospel. I haven't always been in the place I am today. I was raised with that familiar admonition to love the sinner and hate the sin. It was only by taking time to listen to others, to read and to earnestly seek the truth that I have come to see there is no sin in being created homosexual or transgender. Each of us is created as a unique human being, some-one to be affirmed and celebrated. I believe there is nothing in the Scripture to justify our denial of that reality, nothing that condemns anyone in the GLBTQIA community, or any other community, for being who they are.

I am not alone. Millions of Christians love and accept gay, lesbian, bisexual and transgender people as equals in Christ's kingdom. More are being added every day. But that isn't happening by accident. It's happening because we are talking about something that was once taboo. We are dialoguing with people who feel different from us, we are reading the Scriptures anew and we are opening ourselves up to a truth that transcends tradition and accepted social order.

Some of us are part of that change because we have engaged in seeking the truth in a way that has opened us up to the reality of Christ's all-embracing love. Some of you deserve our deepest respect and appreciation because you have found the courage to live your lives and speak your truth even when it was met with violent resistance.

The Good News means that we are called to be partners with God, not by putting on the pretense of seeking after God, but by becoming agents of this change. As we work for repair and restoration we are co-laborers and co-creators with God. We have been empowered to rebuild the ancient ruins. We shall be called Repairers of the Broken Walls. If we believe that God is at work in the world, and if we love God, then we will want to engage in the world, because it is there that God is at work.

There is no secret to what we must do. We must enter into relationship. We must humble ourselves to admit out loud that we do not have all the answers, but we have a willingness to do everything we can to serve the world. We must tell God we are willing to do whatever it takes, including engaging in the transformation of ourselves, to make our witness so real and compelling that through us God can touch the hearts and souls of those who have not heard that they too are beloved.

After twenty-nine years and 6,000 shows, not everyone loved Phil Donohue. That didn't seem to bother him much. In fact, he once said, "I don't see how you can insult me in any original way. I've heard it all."

I have to admit that while I do owe much to Phil Donohue for bringing edgy, contemporary issues to my attention, he can't compare to Jesus when it comes to being controversial or radical. After 2,000 years and innumerable shows, services and rallies, the message of Christianity is every bit as radical as it ever was. If it doesn't sound that way to us today, maybe we just need to turn up the volume or stop changing the channel.

Notes:_____

_____

_____

_____

_____

_____

_____

_____

_____

_____

_____

_____

_____

_____

_____

_____

_____

_____

Feminine and Masculine Energy

Would you rather die having accomplished everything you wanted but without experiencing a truly deep and intimate relationship? Or would you rather die having had an incredibly deep and intimate relationship but not having accomplished anything you wanted?

These questions indicate your dominant sexual energy. There is both masculine and feminine energy, and they have nothing to do with gender. Whether we are heterosexual, homosexual or bisexual, it is helpful to leave behind stereotypical definitions of male and female and to think instead of masculine and feminine energy. Both the masculine and the feminine move within each of us. At the same time, one or the other dominates almost all of us.

If you answered yes to the first question, you have a more masculine essence. If you answered yes to the second question, you have a more feminine essence. Another way to ask the question is this: would you prefer to ravish another or would you rather have another ravish you?

The masculine emphasis is purpose. The feminine emphasis is on connection. Masculine is steady and unchanging. Feminine is creative and flowing from everything else. The masculine drive is for freedom, the feminine for fullness. The masculine fear is losing the self. The feminine fear is losing the other. The feminine grows spiritually by learning to live as love rather than by hoping for it. The masculine grows spiritually by learning to live as freedom rather than by struggling for it. Both paths, that of freedom and that of fullness, lead to spiritual bliss.

Understanding that we all have both feminine and masculine energy allows us to escape the man box and the woman box. The man box defines **men** as domineering, aggressive, competitive, achievement oriented and controlling. Men are providers who offer protection. The woman box defines **women** as nurturing, supportive, passive, sacrificial, giving, and vulnerable. Men are taught that if you move out of the man box you will get labeled from other boxes like the woman box or the gay box. We also teach women that if they move out of the woman box they will be negatively labeled. Men risk being seen as weak and ineffective, of being called "pussy." Woman risk being seen as threatening and unattractive, of being told they have "balls."

When we can claim our own whole identity and grant others permission to be whole human beings, we can celebrate all of our strengths and recognize that the traits we exhibit are present in both men and women alike. Escaping the man box and the woman box offers us liberation from that which oppresses, binds and enslaves. It allows us to become more vulnerable with each other and more open to accepting people as they are.

It is also important to realize we are not frozen or static in our sexual energy. We can and do move back and forth between masculine and feminine as the situation requires and as we are comfortable. For instance, I am in my masculine during my working day. I have to take control and make a lot of decisions, organizing people and situations in order to accomplish specific results. Sometimes, when I return home after a hard day of work, I don't want to make any more decisions. I just want to bask in feminine energy and go with the flow.

Notes:_____

_____

_____

_____

_____

_____

_____

_____

_____

_____

_____

_____

_____

_____

_____

_____

_____

_____

_____

_____

Sexual Attraction

Those energies are also at work every time we make a connection with each other. We feel the arc of sexual attraction when our masculine energy is met by someone's feminine energy, or when our feminine energy is met by someone's masculine energy. That energy can change even within the sex act itself as we move from submission to dominance and back to submission again. As long as we operate in polarities, we find connection and excitement.

Sometimes, we are both operating in the same energy. When we are both in our masculine energy we both want control. When we are both in our feminine our conversation might sound a lot like this:

Me: What do you want to do tonight?

Partner: I don't care. What do you want to do?

Me: I don't know. Maybe we should go out to dinner.

Partner: That's fine. Where do you want to go?

Me: I don't care. Where would you like to go?

When this happens, there is not a lot of excitement. If you are not feeling the arc of sexual attraction to your partner, it's likely you are both in the same energy mode. It's helpful to know that you can change that arc of attraction by switching positions. You can choose to exercise either your feminine or your masculine side and then let the sparks fly.

In our sexual relationships, the joy is that we connect with each other. However, we cannot maintain that connection indefinitely. We cannot lay total claim to each other. There is a sacredness of the other, untouchable and inaccessible, which plunges us into a kind of powerlessness. When we approach that powerlessness with fear, we react in opposite ways. The natural posture for the feminine is to move toward enmeshment.

The natural posture for the masculine is to move into cut off. When these patterns continue, the masculine feels suffocated and trapped while the feminine feels abandoned and lonely.

When we can contain our anxiety and celebrate the unique separateness of our partner, than we can dance between identifying who we are as individuals and staying connected with each other. Then we never need to fear losing our "self," or losing the "other." Then we can celebrate love and experience intimate communion with each other by relaxing into each other and spontaneously offering our deepest gifts.

Notes:_____

_____

_____

_____

_____

_____

_____

_____

_____

_____

_____

_____

_____

_____

_____

_____

_____

_____

_____

_____

_____

Sex Devoid of Spirit

Let me reiterate: I like sex. I think sex is one of the greatest gifts God has given humankind. I like the human body. I like my body. Bodies are good. Sex is good.

It grieves me that the Christian church has for so long preached a separation of body and spirit, a pronouncement against sexuality as a hindrance to ones spiritual growth. By labeling sex as something dirty, the church has robbed countless people of a transcendent experience, a magnificent glimpse into God's own passionate creativity. What a sad, sad state of affairs.

I can think of only one other thing that has so damaged what should be a natural embrace of a full and satisfying sexual life: the sex industry.

Veiled in the disguise of liberation and freedom from sexual repression, the exploitation of human beings has become so pervasive that it has become socially acceptable. It is now a common belief that anyone involved in the sex industry is there by free choice. What was once shocking is now tolerated, and to not tolerate the objectification of human beings, especially of women, is to be labeled a prude.

According to beautyfromashes.org, the sex industry in 2010 was a $97.06 billion worldwide business. Over ten million children work in the sex industry; while between 66% and 90% of those who work in the sex industry were sexually abused as children. While many people would never hire a prostitute or visit a strip club, the pornography industry has exploded. From magazines to DVDs to the internet, the proliferation of pornography has reached staggering levels.

According to crossculturalconnections.org, here are some of the statistics from 2006:

Sex Industry Statistics 2006

$57 billion worldwide/ $12 billion U.S. *(more than the revenues of pro football, baseball and basketball combined)*	Size of Industry
4.2 million	Websites
68 million/day	Search engine requests
116,000/day	Child porn requests
100,000	Websites w/child porn
26	Children's character's names linked to porn sites
11 years	Average age of exposure to internet porn
14 years (49% enter before they are 11 years old)	Average age of entry into prostitution
50%	Percent of music videos on MTV that feature or suggest violence, present hostile sexual situations as acceptable or show male heroes abusing women for fun
4:1	Number of peepshows and adult bookstores in the U.S. compared to the number of McDonald's
1 in 8	Number of Hollywood movies that depict a rape theme

Of course, the sex trade is nothing new. The *Song of Songs* is a moving testament to the power of sexual attraction between partners who are intimate and vulnerable to each other. But the book of *Judges* reminds us of a long history of treating women as property, available to be raped and abused as any man saw fit.

While everyone suffers in this prevailing paradigm, it continues to be women and children who bear the brunt of sexual oppression. Those who suffer sexism, racism, poverty and homelessness, and victims of domestic violence, rape or incest, both at home and abroad are the most vulnerable to such exploitation. And they bear the mighty weight of shame.

Notes:_____

_____

_____

_____

_____

_____

_____

_____

_____

_____

_____

_____

_____

_____

_____

_____

_____

_____

_____

Bound by Shame

Have you ever felt as if there was something happening in your life over which you had no control? Theologian Dietrich Bonhoeffer calls *shame* an impotence-making experience because it feels as though there is no way to relieve the matter, no way to restore the balance of things. There is no single action that is wrong and can be repaired. Shame arises out of the belief that one has simply failed as a human being.

And shame is a binding experience. Shame is the painful feeling of being exposed, being made vulnerable, uncovered and left unprotected, being naked and looked at by others. Shame implies we were at some time vulnerable to the scorn, disrespect and even the hate of another human being, and no repair followed.

Shame leads to self-shaming, to rejecting ourselves before others can reject us. Shame brings distance between people and even within parts of our self. As a result we may find ourselves raging at others, mistrusting people, striving for perfection, struggling for power, and/or internally withdrawing, all in an effort to protect ourselves from further hurt.

It's hard for me to think of anything more binding in our culture today then the painful reality of sexual abuse and the shame that too often results. Any activity that a person feels violates her or his boundaries may fall within the realm of sexual abuse, but there are two primary forms of sexual abuse I will focus on.

One form is any experience during childhood or adolescence that involves inappropriate sexual attention by another person, usually an adult, but sometimes an older child, teenager, or even a same-aged playmate. The behavior may be forced, coerced, or even willingly engaged in by the survivor, but it is understood as abusive because a child **cannot** truly give free consent. The other form is the violent act of rape, including the growing phenomena of date rape. Statistics in both cases are disturbing. According to the latest numbers from RAINN.org, an estimated 17% to 22% of children experience some kind of sexual abuse by the time they are eighteen years old. That is as many as one in three girls and one in six boys. Rape victims are also overwhelmingly young. A full 44% are under 18 years old; 80% are under thirty years old.

Most people who are sexually abused as children or who experience the assault of rape experience difficulties related to the abuse. Rape and molestation victims can experience strong, sometimes crippling emotions, even decades after the event. These emotions include fear, anger and guilt. Victims often live in fear of a recurrence, and that overriding fear often manifests itself in fear of sexual intercourse and/or intimacy with any partner. They often experience anger that can be directed at God, at their molester and/or at people in general. They also tend to feel guilt, believing they are somehow responsible for what happened to them, that they caused the act, didn't fight hard enough or their body betrayed them by responding to the act. These emotions influence behavior, causing irrational, sometimes hostile reactions to natural life situations. Often, a person keeps her or his experience a secret, ashamed and afraid to share this part of their self and their past with others.

I was personally bound for twenty-two years before I could claim publicly that I am a survivor of childhood sexual abuse. I was bound by shame that set in when a traumatic silence followed my abuse. Shame is a binding experience, one that literally cripples children of God. But it is not a life sentence. Even the bonds of shame can be untied.

People who are bound by shame suffer in silence they cannot break. So it is up to us to speak. We need to speak the truth about their experience. We need to say out loud and regularly: you did nothing to deserve sexual abuse. There was nothing in this act that God willed. This abuse hurt God because you are God's precious child. God wants you to be healed, to be loosed from your bonds and to once again stand up straight. You can feel whole, clean and joyful again. Survivors need from us voices that can talk about sexuality in realistic and wholesome terms, voices that can help to find God's grace anew.

If a survivor is able to break his or her own silence, then we need to be able to listen. Victims of sexual abuse struggle with trying to find God in the midst of their horror. We need to listen to their stories if we are to appreciate the reality of that horror and confront the hard questions about sexuality and violence in our culture. More than easy answers, they need us to listen carefully and not assume that we can easily understand their pain and their grief.

If we are to take seriously our task of healing the binding results of abuse, then we cannot only pay attention to individual victims and their recovery. We must act to heal our society. The reality is we live in a rape culture in which primarily women and children receive messages every day that their bodies are meant to be used as commodities and that violations of their bodies will be ignored, tacitly condoned or blamed on them.

It is natural for us to recoil from such a harsh reality, to close our eyes to the pervasiveness and the horror of sexual abuse. It is much more comfortable to redirect our attention to the outward and reprehensible abuses of other people in other lands, such as the Taliban's overt oppression of women or the practice of female circumcision, and deny the cold, hard truth of our own country's atrocities. For such knowledge forces us to question our belief that we are part of a democratic society that is both rational and decent, as well as our desire to believe that all Christians are loving and nice.

We need to face up to the reality and horror of sexualized violence in our lives, not try to cover it up. We need to monitor our own actions, our language and our choices in this life so we do not contribute to a society that continues to harm, to bind and to cripple our sons and our daughters.

We all suffer from a system that exploits and degrades any member of our global family. We are in a difficult position: We believe sex is good, but not always, not under any circumstance. Thomas Moore in his book *Soul Mates* writes, "It would help if we would stop thinking of sex as something strictly physical. Because in truth the whole sphere of sex – emotion, body, fantasy, and relationship – falls within the domain of the soul."

Notes:_____

_____

_____

_____

_____

_____

_____

_____

_____

_____

_____

_____

_____

_____

_____

_____

_____

Claiming Our Sexuality

Each of us has a sexual history, for good or for ill. We may also have strong sexual hopes and longings. These images are creations of the soul. The memory of a pleasurable experience may carry longings about pleasure in life itself, while a painful memory may color our world with disillusion and hopelessness. Our image of ourselves as lovers may be wrapped up in these memories. So may fear of exposure of the parts of us we try to hide and deny.

Sex asks something of us: that we live more fully and manifest ourselves more transparently. The intimacy in sex, while always attached to the body, is never only physical. Sex brings up in us stories, emotions and fragments of our past. Our sexuality says something about us, and it says something about our soul. We can exploit sex, manipulate others with it, use it with fierce aggression, hide from it, or indulge excessively in it. But if we let it, the soul of sex can inspire relationship, sustain it, and make it worthwhile. We are asked to stand out of the way and to be affected by its power to transform us.

God save us from the kind of conservativism that strangles the passion out of life and would seek to teach us that sex is somehow ungodly and unclean. How grateful we should be that we need no longer cower in the sexual repression of past generations. We are free to love our bodies, to relish sex and to marvel in this good gift from God.

But God also save us from the kind of liberalism that teaches that my actions are mine alone, that I have no responsibility for the darkness in society, that I am not intimately connected to every human being on this planet, that each fate is not also mine to bear. And finally God restore to us the joy of being a body fully united to spirit, the wonder of being a truly whole and holy person.

Namaste

Notes:_____

_____

_____

_____

_____

_____

_____

_____

_____

_____

_____

_____

_____

_____

_____

_____

_____

_____

_____

_____

_____

_____

_____

_____

_____

_____

_____

_____

_____

_____

_____

_____

_____

_____

_____

_____

_____

_____

_____

_____